YOUR KNOWLEDGE HAS VALUE

Irina Giertz

British Drama of the 90s

In-yer-face theatre

GRIN Publishing

Bibliographic information published by the German National Library:

The German National Library lists this publication in the National Bibliography; detailed bibliographic data are available on the Internet at http://dnb.dnb.de .

Imprint:

Copyright © 2005 GRIN Verlag GmbH
Print and binding: Books on Demand GmbH, Norderstedt Germany
ISBN: 978-3-656-85127-1

This book at GRIN:

http://www.grin.com/en/e-book/285210/british-drama-of-the-90s

GRIN - Your knowledge has value

Since its foundation in 1998, GRIN has specialized in publishing academic texts by students, college teachers and other academics as e-book and printed book. The website www.grin.com is an ideal platform for presenting term papers, final papers, scientific essays, dissertations and specialist books.

Visit us on the internet:

http://www.grin.com/

http://www.facebook.com/grincom

http://www.twitter.com/grin_com

British Drama of the 90s

Essay

Anthony Neilson *Penetrator* (1993)

Harry Gibson *Trainspotting* (1994)

Sarah Kane *Blasted* (1995)

Mark Ravenhill *Shopping and Fucking* (1996)

Partick Marber *Closer* (1997)

Rebecca Prichard *Yard Gal* (1998)

Sarah Kane *Cleansed* (1998)

Joe Penhall *Blue Orange* (2001)

1. <u>What is in-yer-face theatre?</u>

    1.1. Characteristics of in-yer-face theatre: sensation, shock, confrontation, taboo breaking, disturbing, provocative, attacking

    1.2. Distinguishing elements: language, themes, taboo words, nudity, sex scenes, disgust, pain

    1.3. Immediacy of theatre performance

2. <u>The history of provocative theatre</u>

    2.1. Ancient Greek Theatre

    2.2. Jacobean Theatre

    2.3. Experimental Theatre from 1960s

    2.4. Censorship

3. <u>How in-yer-face theatre works (principles, techniques, themes, formal structure)</u>

    3.1. *Shopping and Fucking*

    3.2. *Blasted*

References:

Siertz, Aleks. 2000. *In-Yer-Face Theatre. British Drama Today.*

Innes, Christopher. 1992. *Modern British Drama.* 1890-1990. Cambridge UP.

1. What is in-yer-face theatre?

"The wildest definition of in-yer-face theatre is any drama that takes the audience by the scruff of the neck and shakes it until it gets the message." (Aleks Siertz)

The most frequently used characteristics of in-yer-face theatre are sensation, shock, confrontation, taboo breaking, disturbing, provocative, attacking. It is a theatre of **sensation**, both actors and spectators are kicked out of the orbit/domain of conventional reactions, touches nerves, provokes alarm. Often such dramas employ **shock** tactics, or is shocking because it is new in tone or structure, or because it is more experimental than what the audience is used to. It questions **moral norms** and affronts the dominating ideas of what can or should be shown onstage. It also works with more primitive feelings, smashing **taboos**, mentioning the forbidden, creating discomfort.

How can one tell if a play is in-yer-face? It isn't really difficult. The language is usually filthy, characters talk about unmentionable subjects, take their clothes off, have sex, humiliate each other, experience unpleasant emotions, become suddenly violent. The audience exposed to such scenes where it plays the part of the voyeur feels duly uncomfortable and uneasy and is forced to react, they either leave the theatre immediately, or are convinced that it is the best thing they have ever seen. This kind of theatre usually inspires to use superlatives, whether in praise or condemnation.

Shock is a way to wake up the audience since the plays deal with disturbing subjects and explore difficult feelings. Through such provocations and confrontations writers intend to push the boundaries of what is acceptable. They question current ideas of what is normal, what it means to be human, what is natural and what is real. In other words, they use shock as part of a search for deeper meaning, as well as part of a rediscovery of theatrical possibilities, to see just how far they can go.

There can be distinguished **the hot and the cool versions** of in-yer-face theatre. The hot version is often performed in smaller theatres and uses the aesthetics of extremism: the language is blatant, the action explicit, the emotions heightened. The aggression is open and the experience remains unforgettable. Cooler versions appear more distanced in comparison. They are played to a larger audience, are more traditional in structure and means. Comedy is often used to ease unpleasant feelings since laughter is a common reaction to terror (the other is ignoring it).

Most in-yer-face theatre **challenges the distinctions we use to define who we are**: human vs. animal, clean vs. dirty, healthy vs. unhealthy, normal vs. abnormal, good vs. evil, right vs. wrong, just vs. unjust. These binary opposition are central to our world view – so questioning them can be very unsettling. However, only by seeing the other side of all things "good" and by comparing them can we better realise what we really are and what our "goodness" is worth. Therefore, this type of theatre forces us to face ideas and feelings we would normally avoid because they are too painful, too frightening, too unpleasant, or too acute. They remind us of the awful things human being are capable of and of the limits of our self-control. In theatre we can safely explore such emotions. Thus, it is the violation of this sense of safety that makes the experimental theatre so powerful.

Provocative: either unconventional subject matter in conventional structure (the well-made play), or more traditional subjects in an unfamiliar theatrical structure.

How can theatre be so shocking? The main reason is its immediacy and live character. When we are watching a play, it is mostly in real time with real people acting in the same room. So when we find ourselves reacting and others are reacting too, and are aware of our reaction. So subjects that might be bearable when we read about them in private suddenly seem disturbing when shown in public. Situations that are essentially private, such as sex, seem embarrassingly intimate onstage. When taboos are broken in public, the spectators often become complicit witnesses.

Moreover, live performances heighten awareness, increase potential embarrassment, and can make the representation of private pain on a public stage almost unbearable. The audience does not know how far the action will go to shock it and there is always the risk that something unexpected might happen since every performance is different. This increases the tension.

Theatre depends not only on the suspension of disbelief but also on **empathy**. Although no one believes in what is shown onstage, many spectators invest emotionally in it. Although what is shown is make-believe, they take it close to their hearts.

Words seem to cause more offence than the acts to which they refer. **Taboo words**, such as 'fuck' and 'cunt', work because we give them certain magic power which makes them more than simple signs that describe an event or a thing. Like all taboo words, they are a way of guarding against imagined infections, a way of drawing a line that must not be crossed. Swear words become a verbal act of aggression, and in theatre, where they are used openly, they appear even stronger.

Nudity onstage is more powerful than nudity in other visual media because the real person is actually present. Moreover, nudity is often culturally loaded with metaphorical significance, it can be an act of power or an expression of helplessness, etc.

What most **affronts** us can sometimes be what most **fascinates** us. Because in-yer-face theatre treats difficult subjects, it touches what we want to know about ourselves but are too afraid to find out. The public staging of secret desires and monstrous acts both repels us and draws us in.

Disgust – new source of catharsis in the 20th century through fear and disgust, both emotions are linked to taboos of sex and death

Fear of random violence, distinctions between public and private spheres are blurred

Disgust – border concept: marks the border between 'me' and 'the other', "the abject has to be othered" (Julia Kristeva "The Abject", "Powers of Horror" 1980)

from 1980's onwards disgust has been used in art to attack the ego boundaries, to shock since the shock threshold has become lower

Pain – predominant emotion; ways to overcome it; is the end of pain death?

the only way to connect to reality

other aspects of pain - violence to others/oneself – pity/emotion; is pain part of compassion?

2. The history of provocative theatre

In-yer-face drama looks back on a rich history of theatre of provocation.

The greatest of the **ancient Greek** tragedies deal with extreme states of mind: brutal death and terrible suicides, agonising pain and dreadful suffering, human sacrifice, cannibalism, rape, incest, mutilation and humiliation. Most tragedies are built on the waywardness of fate and most intimate fears. Their intention was to purge the bad feelings of the audience. The idea of putting yourself through hell in order to exorcise your inner demons is at the root of experimental theatre.

The **Jacobean theatre** deals with horrible murders, painful tortures, wanton acts of cruelty and vicious vengeance. Murder is depicted in all details, with mutilations, incest. Audience was delighted by horrible stage images and thrilled by depictions of evil. To the end of the play all wrong-doers are dead – the triumph of justice in the 'tragedy of blood'. It was the expectation that morality (Christian moral) would be finally restored that gave the audience permission to enjoy such unnatural acts. John Webster *The Dutchess of Malfi*, John Ford *'Tis Pity She's a Whore* (1633).

However, uncontrolled emotions were often seen as dangerous, and the best way of making theatre safe for audiences was **censorship**. Introduced in Britain in 1737, strict rules have been controlling the nation's stages. The Lord Chamberlain read and licensed all plays, forbidding the showing of material that was indecent, blasphemous or otherwise offensive. The list of things banned included swearwords; nudity; risqué stage business; representations of God, the Royal family or anyone living; and homosexuality. Victorian and Edwardian theatre was censored even stricter. As late as 1909, Edward Garnett could not describe the condition of the heroine of his play as 'pregnant' because it was considered vulgar and likely to inflame lascivious thoughts. He had to use the French word 'enceinte'; if you were classy enough to speak French, presumably you were immune to sudden lust.

The early **sixties** saw the emergence of a truly confrontational theatre in Britain. Inspired by Antonin Artaud ('The Theatre of Cruelty: First Manifesto' 1932 – "the truthful precipitates of dreams"), Jerzy Grotowski, Herman Nitsch (Theatre of Orgy and Hysteria, rituals, from the use of blood and excrement through disgust to catharsis), Peter Brook founded together with Charles Marowitz an experimental group **'Theatre of Cruelty'**. Brook's innovation is based on the ancient Greek theatre, Shakespeare, non-european theatre, rituals, collective experiment as well as exposition of human body. One of the most articulate productions of Brook's workshop was *Marat-Sade* (1964) after the play by Peter Weiss *The Persecution and Assassination of Marat as Performed by the Inmates of the Asylum of Charenton under the Direction of the Marquis de Sade*, which also served as a plot summary for the piece (joke!). Artaud's concept of 'cruelty', however, had less to do with sadism than with the exploration of the possibilities of the actors' bodies, their non-verbal resources, to regain the absolute freedom of expression onstage, like a writer when experiencing on paper. The ultimate aim was to purge Western society of its materialistic morality, to reach the audience directly through a 'necessary cruelty' in exposing the audience to deliberate violence. The expressive means employed breaking all sorts of taboos like nudity, close bodily contact, shouting, spitting, imitation of defecation, copulation, imitation of blood or excrement, etc. were extremely unsettling for the audience. However, these rituals were set within an explicitly theatrical frame.

(Theater of the Absurd: power is the subject matter – dominance, control, exploitation, subjugation, victimisation; Beckett, Harold Pinter *The Caretaker*, Tom Stoppard)

Quite a number of plays in the 1960's were outrageous in their content which moved Lord Chamberlain to abolish censorship in 1968. Besides the *Angry Young Men* plays and *Kitchen Sink Dramas* which expressed social anger among the working class, the poor and the disadvantaged (John Osborne *Look Back in Anger* 1956, Arnold Wesker, John Arden, Edward Bond), there are other, more brutal plays. David Rudkin's work aimed to exorcise unconscious demons by assaulting audience sensibilities. His plays show animal copulation, guards sodomising prisoners, dismemberment, demented and deformed characters, and other mutilations. Edward Bond's *Saved* includes the scene where a baby in a pram is stoned to death by a gang of youths. Joe Orton's *Entertaining Mr. Sloane* (1964) and *Loot* (1966) affront the audience by the explicit treating of incest.

Political and social issues, racism of the plays' content were juxtaposed with the images of nakedness, perversities, violence, the cacophony of sounds.

Post-dramatic theatre

3. How in-yer-face theatre works (principles, techniques, themes, formal structure)

In the 90's theatre broke all taboos, very many plays were blatant, aggressive and emotionally dark. The extreme sides were focused upon, themes were taken to the limit: if drama dealt with masculinity, it showed rape; if violence was wanted, torture was staged. The language was often gross, the jokes sick, the images indelible. The cruelty onstage was matter-of-fact and common. Nudity ceased to be only a symbol of liberation, it became more problematic, often associated with vulnerability.

Innovations in structure, highly explicit stage pictures.

The recipe for a new kind of theatre was: subvert the idea of a coherent character; turn scenes into flexible scenarios; substitute brief messages for text; mix clever dialogue with brutal images; stage the show as an art installation.

<u>Themes</u>: sexuality, violence, nudity, drugs; refusal the moral values, search for the meaning of life

Britain was seen as a bleak place where young people were foul-mouthed and irreverent, wildly gleeful and often hip, lonely, exasperated, aggressive, in short – troubled. Such characters inhabited episodic stories rather than three-act plots, metaphor-rich situations rather than well-made plays.

<u>Formal structure:</u>

The question of structure reflects the way how reality is seen.

<u>plot</u> – instead of a plot in the sense of a well-made play they have a strong sense of experiential confrontation,

<u>language</u> – instead of long speeches curt televisual dialogue, strikes by its vitality and immediacy which recall and mimic real speech without being either documentary or realistic; the dialogue is faster, the exchanges sharper, the expressions of emotions more direct and extreme, the language is more highly coloured

<u>characters</u> – no complex characters/individuals but types, however there is no simplification: characters are contradictory

<u>content</u> – instead of a naturalistic content of a well-made play worlds beyond mere realism, instead of moral ambiguity of a well-made play unresolved contradictions.

This imaginary Britain was of course much darker than the real, it was more raw, savage and critical. The exaggeration was meant to stir up the audience and to remind them of extreme experiences which were taking place elsewhere. Kane: "I'd rather risk overdose in the theatre than in life".

<u>Principles</u>: the motives behind the provocation were not to titillate with ugly scenes and deeply disturbing situations, but to spread knowledge of what humans are capable of; complacency came under fire everywhere, the new theatre was there to question ideas in such a way as to make audiences uncomfortable; however, the nineties drama refrained from giving solutions out of a conscious decision not to preach to audiences.

<u>Techniques</u>: a twofold strategy between involvement and distance, with no oscillating movement between them; showing emotions – what can affect the audience, how? Two major emotions – fear and disgust (cf. Greek theatre: fear and pity/terror), the strongest

feelings, linked to taboos (sex and death)

Disgust is caused by showing bodily fluids and excrements, as well as bodily functions

Criticism: Where is the line between provocation and sensationalism? (imitations of Tarantino) If the audiences' attention can only be held by violence and lewdness, doesn't the ensuing insensitivity demand more and more violence and lewdness? In this case, it leads to loss of humanity.

Lack of compassion – prohibits identification with characters, watching plays feels alienating, the inherent humanity obscured behind the dialogue should be exposed by the directors.

The new plays and writers were hyped, spin doctors and media coverage provided good advertisment, theatres applied new marketing strategies to promote the new plays. Despite of the first reviews, the new writing turned commercial. There were fashionable topics each year – either heroine, or gangster stories, etc. At the same time, the nineties saw a great liberation of the imagination of British dramatists. This explosion of confrontational drama saved theatre at a time when it risked becoming wholly irrelevant to the wider culture.

At the same time, this theatre has redefined the notion of beauty, ideas of what can or cannot be said and shown.

In-yer-face theatre can be described as an arena, an imaginary place that can be visited or passed through, a spot where a writer can grow up, or where they can return to after other adventures.

Shopping and Fucking (1996) – Mark Ravenhill

The trouble with the title: *Shopping and F***ing, Shopping and*

Themes: sex, homosexuality, drugs, selling and consuming, sexual violence, rape, incest, humiliation, telephone sex, Diana and Fergie, dependencies – emotional and drug induced, identity (crisis, masculine)

"Civilisation is money. Money is civilisation"

Formal structure: traditional plot, metaphors of shopping and fucking throughout the play, telling tales

Techniques: the action (sex, eating, shopping, drug-dealing, help) is mainly described as transaction, without personal emotions involved

Principles: Extreme characters pushed to extreme situations. The market had filtered into every aspect of their lives. Sex, which should have been private, had become a public transaction.

Closer (1997) - **Partick Marber**

Themes: identity, self-definition through telling stories which are endlessly mutable, picking up others' identities, the truth about one's identity, search for authenticity; love, relationships, swapping partners, irrationality of desire, unreasonable passions, truth in the relationships; stereotypes and role models in the representation of men and women, crisis of masculinity

Formal structure: realistic, recognisable representation, patterns, identifiable characters; structure of the tragedy with the climax and tragic outcome

Techniques: very explicit language, pornographic fantasies in the Internet scene; taboo breaking is more subtle

Yard Gal (1998) - Rebecca Prichard

<u>Themes</u>: girl's play, 'black' subculture (race issue is not decisive), violence between women, community spirit, gangs fights, initiation rites (tattoo), unconscious imitation of male patterns, violence and fears are talked about; drugs; commitment, friendship

<u>Formal structure</u>: conventional structure – exposition (establishing the characters and scene), climax (crime and imprisoning), and consequences (letters); inside acts are series of narrations

<u>Techniques</u>: addressing the audience directly in order to involve the audience, self-reference of the characters; story telling; no violence onstage, only verbal violence; comedy elements made the characters more humane

Penetrator (1993) – Anthony Neilson

<u>Themes</u>: a boy's play, homoeroticism – ambiguous, sex connected with violence ("I want you to shoot me"), repression – sexual and emotional venting in violence, violence as the only reaction to the world

Tadge is based on a real person, psychopathic tendencies due to incomplete childhood

the knife sequence – a carthatic experience

teddy's disemboweling – destruction of childhood

<u>Formal structure</u>: traditional, plot – "a romantic triangle", centered on the fear of the inexplicable, of violence

Trainspotting (1994) - Harry Gibson

Novel by Irvine Welsch (1993), adapted for the screen in 1996

Themes: drugs, soccer, sex, music, boredom and lack of excitement, heroine as excitement, violence towards women and women's revenge (misogynist play, boy's play) no real emotions, no communication except that through drugs

Formal structure: no plot, the play is hold together by images and metaphors – heroine, trainspotting = 'tracks'

mixture of comedy and despair and bleakness

four actors share different roles, transforms multiple viewpoint

novel – eight first person narrators, shifts of perspective

no explanation

no moral judgement

Blasted (1995) – Sarah Kane

Blasted is Kane's first play, written at 23, and the play which marked the new period in British theatre.

Plot: in a very expensive hotel room in Leeds, Ian, a middle-aged journalist, stays with Cate, a naïve vulnerable young woman prone to epileptic fits, and rapes her eventually; suddenly a soldier appears, urinates on the bed; then the hotel is blasted apart by a bomb; the soldier rapes Ian, sucks out his eyes, eats them and shoots himself; Cate returns with a baby which dies and Cate buries it under the floorboards; after she leaves to get some food Ian masturbates, defecates and eats the baby; by now he is under the floorboards, with only his head poking out; he dies; Cate returns with provisions.

The play immediately became the focus of the most aggressive reviews of the decade and the centre of the biggest scandal.

Themes: sex and violence, tenderness and violence, hope and love, war (in Bosnia), crisis of masculinity; also: guilt, sickness, men-women relationship, sexuality, self-destruction, death, verbal violence, cannibalism, tribalism, childhood, innocence, cleanness, nudity, social class

<u>Formal structure</u>: slapstick elements livens the play up, mixture between atrocities and comic, two obviously separate parts – a drawing room comedy with private, gendered verbalised violence and war, "public" violence transferred to the private sphere where the atrocities from the first part are now visualised

<u>Principles</u>: atrocities have to be shown onstage, not offstage, however not naturalistic, but symbolic, metaphoric; no message but connections between private violence and war violence, between maleness and violence, logical conclusions; images are concrete, not ideologically biased (masculinity)

Cleansed (1998) – Sarah Kane

"Chopping and fucking"

A group of inmates of a certain institution called niversity try to save themselves through love. Defies easy summary. The main story-line is about Grace looking for Graham, her brother, an addict who has been murdered by Tinker, a sadistic guard or doctor. Grace wear Graham's clothes, makes love to his spirit and finally get a penis transplant and becomes him. Juxtaposed with this story of incest and sibling bonding is the romance of two men, Carl and Rod, who discuss love and betrayal. Carl, who promises eternal love, betrays his lover; Rod, who lives for a moment, dies for love. In a subplot, Robin, a disturbed 19-year-old, falls for Grace when she tries to teach him to read, and hangs himself. The last story: Tinker visits a peepshow and imposes Grace's identity onto that of the erotic dancer, he seduces her and turns nasty. At the end the roles are swapped.

<u>Themes</u>: love, addiction, loss, need, suffering, despair, gender, identity, purification and redemption ; Tinker reduces the possibilities of others to love, torturer or cataliser; Tinker's gaze – control, power, but also desire;

Formal structure: four interweaving story lines coming together at the end

Techniques: vivid images; atrocities are shown deliberately unrealistic; blood, rats, fire are shown through symbolic things; naturalistic scenes are avoided; relations are symbolic: the incestuous, identity-sharing twins; the classic couple with one idealistic and another realistic; domination and alienated love; a teacher and pupil, mother and child rapport

Principles: catharsis, cleansing = punishment, coming through pain to love; losing and finding oneself again

Blue Orange (2001) - Joe Penhall

Themes: race, racism (institutionalised), madness (Borderline Personality Disorder), normality, power struggle, manipulation

Formal structure: conventional plot